Brave Little Squirrel

Md. Ziaul Haque

Copyright © 2024 Md. Ziaul Haque

All rights reserved.

ISBN: 9798326990006

Reasons behind Penning this Book

Brave Little Squirrel is a captivating collection of nursery rhymes carefully curated for young readers. Featuring an array of diverse topics, this delightful book provides children with a whimsical journey through the world of imagination and wonder. From charming tales of animals in the forest to magical adventures in far-off lands, each rhyme is intricately crafted to engage young minds and spark their creativity.

With vibrant illustrations that bring each rhyme to life, *Brave Little Squirrel* is sure to enchant both children and parents alike. Perfect for bedtime reading or quiet moments of reflection, this beautifully illustrated book is a timeless addition to any child's library. Join *Brave Little Squirrel* on its enchanting adventures as you explore the joy and magic of childhood through the pages of this charming collection of nursery rhymes!

Brave Little Squirrel

Dedication

To my lovely wife Farmina Taslim and our cute princess Azmiran Haq!

Contents

1	Friendly Frog	10
2	Bumblebee's Song	11
3	Little Red Wagon	12
4	Giggle Twins	13
5	Sleepy Owl	14
6	Happy Caterpillar	15
7	Tiny Tugboat	16
8	Dancing Dandelion	17
9	Little Star	18
10	Brave Little Squirrel	19

Brave Little Squirrel

Friendly Frog

In a pond so clear and bright,
Lived a frog who leaped with might.
He sang a tune both day and night,
And danced beneath the moon's soft light.

With lily pads and flowers sweet,
He splashed around with nimble feet.
He made new friends, a joyful feat,
In the pond where they would meet.

Hoppy, hoppy, jump so high,
The friendly frog leaps to the sky!

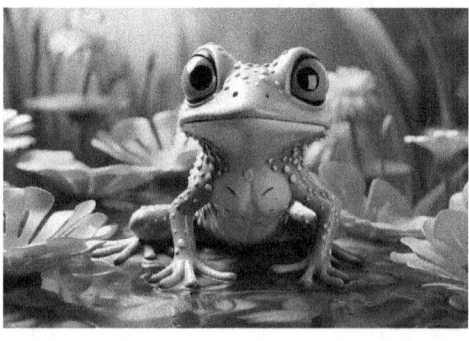

Bumblebee's Song

Bumblebee, oh bumblebee,
Buzzing through the blossomed tree.
With your stripes of black and gold,
Stories of the flowers told.

Gathering nectar all the day,
Flying in a zigzag way.
Spreading pollen here and there,
Blooming beauty everywhere.

Buzz, buzz, buzzing by,
Bumblebee in the summer sky.

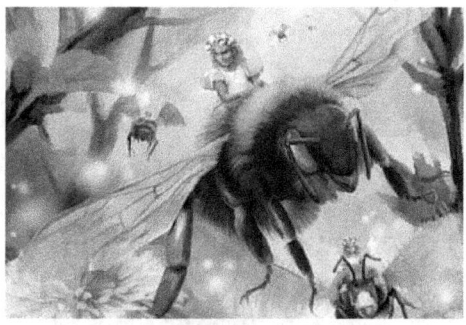

Little Red Wagon

Roll along, my little red wagon,
With a teddy bear and a dragon.
We'll go down the bumpy road,
Sharing stories, light and load.

Through the meadow, past the brook,
Every corner we will look.
Finding treasures, big and small,
Adventures waiting for us all.

Rolling, rolling, off we go,
With my red wagon in tow.

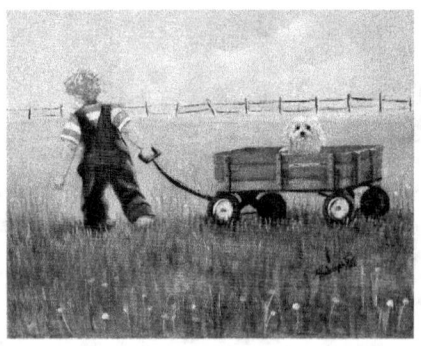

Giggle Twins

Giggle twins with sunny grins,

Playing games where fun begins.

Hide and seek or jump and hop,

Laughing loud, they never stop.

In the garden, down the lane,

Skipping ropes and dancing in rain.

Every day a brand new game,

Joy and laughter they proclaim.

Giggling, giggling, all the way,

The twins make every day a play.

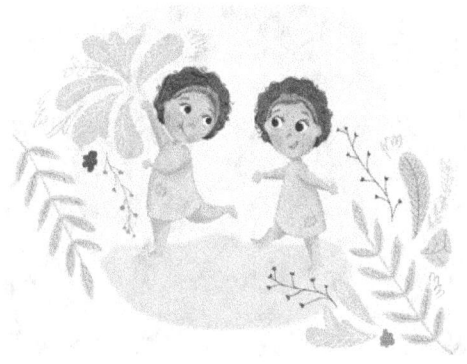

Sleepy Owl

In a tree so tall and high,

Lived an owl who loved the sky.

During day, he'd close his eyes,

Waiting for the moon to rise.

When the stars began to gleam,

He awoke from daytime dream.

Hooting softly in the night,

Guided by the pale moonlight.

Sleepy, sleepy, in the day,

Owl wakes up when night's at play.

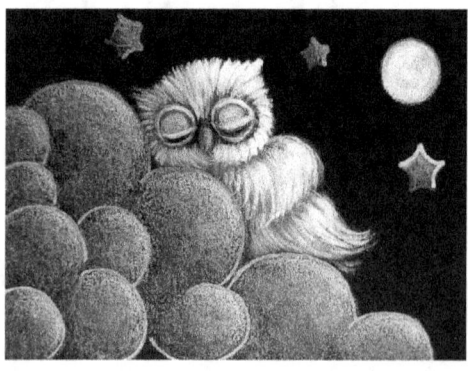

Happy Caterpillar

Caterpillar, small and green,

In the garden, often seen.

Munching leaves and growing strong,

Knowing he won't stay there long.

Building up his cozy home,

In his chrysalis alone.

Time will pass, and he will fly,

As a butterfly in the sky.

Creeping, creeping, then so high,

Caterpillar waves goodbye.

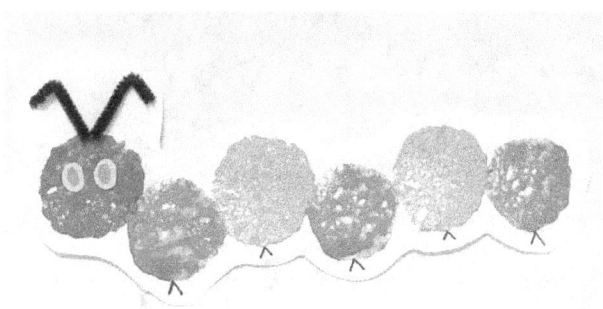

Tiny Tugboat

Tiny tugboat in the bay,
Pulling ships throughout the day.
Whistles loud and engines strong,
Helping all the boats along.

Through the waves and through the tide,
Tugging with a steady stride.
When the sun begins to set,
Homeward bound, no regrets.

Tugging, tugging, here and there,
Tiny tugboat everywhere.

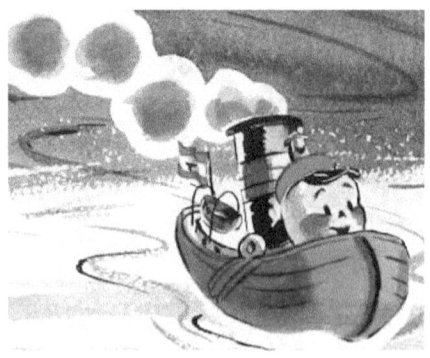

Dancing Dandelion

Dandelion in the breeze,
Dancing with the greatest ease.
Golden petals in the sun,
Spinning, twirling, having fun.

When the wind begins to blow,
Seeds are carried to and fro.
Planting dreams in fields anew,
Waiting for the morning dew.

Dancing, dancing, light and free,
Dandelion wild and free.

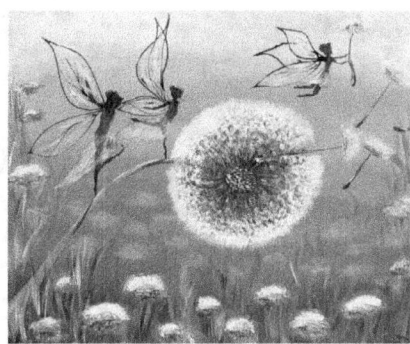

Little Star

Twinkle, twinkle, little star,
Shining brightly from afar.
High above the world so high,
Like a diamond in the sky.

Guiding travelers through the night,
With your gentle, gleaming light.
Wishing upon your spark so bright,
Dreams take flight in pure delight.

Twinkling, twinkling, up so high,
Little star lights up the sky.

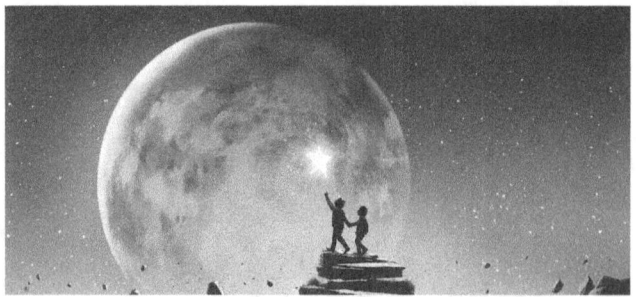

Brave Little Squirrel

In the forest, up a tree,
Lived a squirrel, wild and free.
Brave and bold, he'd leap and bound,
Gathering acorns all around.

In his cozy nest he'd stay,
Through the night and through the day.
With his bushy tail so bright,
Facing every little fright.

Leaping, leaping, tree to tree,
Brave little squirrel, full of glee.

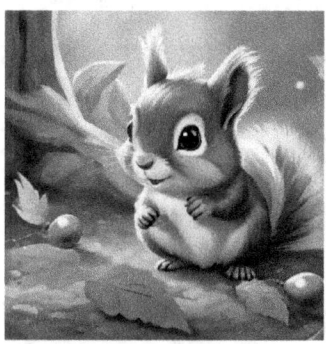

About the Author

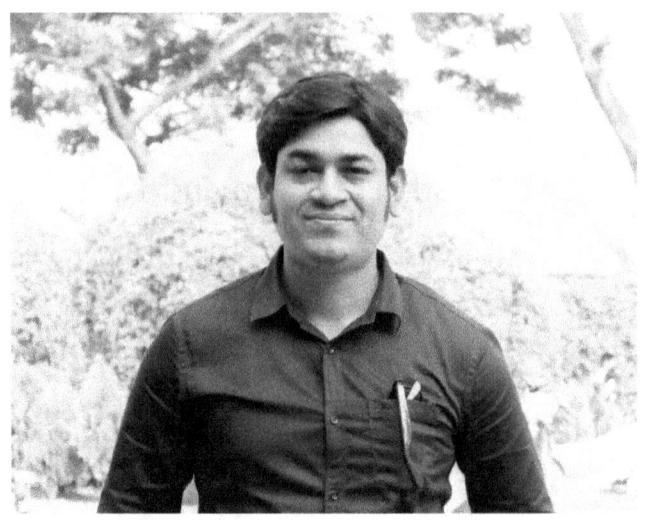

Md. Ziaul Haque, born and raised in Bangladesh, is a multi-talented individual known for his contributions to various artistic fields. With an extensive list of accomplishments, he has earned recognition as an international award-winning poet, writer, novelist, dramatist, actor, director, academic, songwriter, essayist, researcher, and scholar.

Haque's academic journey began at Shah Jalal University of Science & Technology in Sylhet, where he pursued his Bachelor's and Master's degrees in English Language and Literature. He later expanded his horizons by becoming an alumnus of George Mason University in America, enhancing his knowledge and skills in his chosen fields of study.

Using the pen name 'Shobdoraj,' which translates to 'King of Words' in English, Haque has captivated readers and audiences alike with his profound literary works. Readers have affectionately bestowed him with the titles of 'The Poet of Creativity' and 'The Great Poet' in recognition of his talent and contributions to the literary world.

Haque's writings have graced the pages of renowned national and international literary journals, newspapers, and magazines. His thought-provoking poetry, engaging essays, and captivating stories have found their way into the hearts and minds of readers worldwide.

Beyond his remarkable literary achievements, Haque has made significant contributions to the world of language and literature. He has invented numerous words, terms, and literary forms, pushing the boundaries of creativity and innovation. Some of his notable creations include "Poetenry" [poems of ten lines], "Kurine" [poems of twenty lines], "Distant-author" [a writer who is currently a citizen of another country but writes about his motherland and its people, culture etc.], "Prosaic-ideas" [ideas in brain appear in prosaic forms, they do not normally follow any metrical composition], "Translation of Objects" [in literary works, objects can also be translated and mistranslated since they are considered as equivalents to something else], "Post-postmodern Age" [the proposed name of the era after Post-modernism as the writer mentioned in a newspaper article], "Intentional Delay of Vision" [not seeing or avoiding the reality intentionally], "Jealouty" [jealousy + beauty]- [a feeling of being jealous of another person's beauty or handsomeness; in Bangla, Porosrikatorota], "Inextrovert" [introvert + extrovert]- [a person who is normally quiet or shy and feels uneasy to talk to other people but sometimes becomes friendly and likes the company of others], "Kidultnap" [kid + adult + nap]- [the action of taking away both kids and adults by force to detain them as prisoners and demand money from their family members for returning them], "Foolligent" [fool + intelligent]- [a person who behaves foolishly sometimes but acts intelligently in certain circumstances; foolish but sometimes intelligent], defined the word "Simplex" in a new way- [Simple + Complex = Simplex]- [A problem or something else that seems simple but is complex actually], "A Writer's Religious Partiality" [A writer's religious partiality becomes clear when he chooses the names of the characters for most of his stories, novels etc. from his own religion], "Prosetic" [Prosaic + Poetic]- [A poem that is prosaic in form but looks poetic also since it has rhymes], "Consequential Colonialism" [The names of places of the colonised countries that remind the local citizens about the colonial moments of the past], "Smellwitness" [A person who has smelt something and is able to tell about it to others], "Poeten"- [The poet who writes only ten-line-poems], "Poestory" [Poetry + Story]-

[A new genre of writing in literature that is created by blending two words i.e. poetry + story. In a word, it is a type of writing where a story has both the qualities of poetry and prose; in Bangla- Golpita], "Prosetry" [Prose + Poetry]- [Having the qualities of both prose and poetry], "Death-vision in the Objects and Minor Accidents"- [Objects and minor accidents that sometimes indicate at bigger and terrible accidents where people may die], "Haqueian Verse" [A new form of poetry created by me is called 'Haqueian Verse', which starts with a single word; it has five lines that contain ten words in total. The poem ends with a single word that rhymes with the first word], "Murder Committed by Using Words and Gestures" [Iago drives Othello towards the point of insanity by spreading rumour about Desdemona. He suffers psychologically as his honour is at a stake and his self-respect is ruined. As a result, Othello murders his wife; Broadly, Iago commits the murder of Desdemona and Othello by using his cunning words and gestures.], "Deathreat" or "Dethreat" [An expression of intention to murder someone; a threat by one person or a group of people to kill another person or group of people.], "Philogy" [Philogy is a mixture of two words- Philosophy and Logic. It means the study of philosophy and logic at the same time. In other words, it is the branch of knowledge that deals with philosophy and logic.], "Philogical" [Philogical is a mixture of two words- Philosophical and Logical. It means an idea, expression or thought that is philosophical and logical at the same time.], "Medition" [Medition is a noun and verb. It is a mixture of two words- Medicine + Meditation. As a noun, it means the action or practice of meditating or meditioning by taking some friendly medicines or drugs that have no side-affects. It is the act of taking some legal or less harmful drugs and giving one's attention to only one thing as a way of becoming calm and relaxed. However, the drugs are not allowed in the religious meditations; as a verb, it means to take harmless drugs and think deeply about something. It also means to take drugs that have no side-affects and think calm thoughts in order to relax. However, drugs are not allowed in religious kinds of meditations.], "Shakespeareius" [It is a noun and adjective; a mixture of two words- Shakespeare + Genius. As a noun, it means someone who has William Shakespeare's exceptional, intellectual or creative power in him; as an adjective, it means a person, ideas, writings, thoughts etc. have the qualities or characteristics of William Shakespeare or his writings], "Fiverse" [Five + Verse: Poems of Five Lines, a new poetic form created or invented by me. In Bangla, it is called Panchpodee Kobita. There are 5 lines and total 15 words in it. 1st line has 1 word; 2nd line has 2 words; 3rd line has 3 words; 4th line has 4 words and 5th line has 5 words. 1st line rhymes with the 2nd line; 3rd line is unrhymed; 4th and 5th lines rhyme with each other. The rhyme scheme is: AABCC. There are no punctuation marks at the end of the lines], "Powery" ['Powery' is an adjective that is similar to 'powerful'. It means having great power or strength.], "Songer" [A songer is a person who writes songs or lyrics. It also means a person who writes popular songs or the music for them.], "Tennet" [Poems of Ten Lines], "Ellian" [The teachers, students, researchers, things etc. of English Language and Literature (ELL)], "Chattogramian" [A person from Chattogram, which is a port-city in Bangladesh. Belonging to or relating to Chattogram or its people. The city was previously called Chittagong.], "Sporshophone" [That is what he calls the 'Touch Phone' in Bangla]. "Powery" ['Powery' is an adjective that is similar to 'powerful'. It means having great power or strength.], "Platonisexual Love" ['Platonic Love' is a close relationship between two persons where sexual desire does not exist or has been suppressed or sublimated. The unification of the souls is important, not the bodies. The souls are attracted to each other rather than the bodies. However, 'Platonisexual Love' is an affectionate relationship where the souls of the lovers are united and sexuality is also present. For example, the love between the husband and wife, and the lover and beloved. If the souls of the spouses are one, then it is 'Platonic'; if they have a physical relationship, then it is 'sexual'- Platonisexual.], "Realies" ['Real' plus 'Lies': A real, not playfully said, false statement that is intentionally presented as being true.], "Smartty" [Smart + Witty]: Displaying or described by fast and creative verbal and written humour.

In addition to his creative endeavors, Haque enjoys playing chess, indulging in good music, angling, and occasional theatre directing. He also maintains an active presence on various social networking sites, allowing him to connect with friends and readers.

While Haque remains a dreamer at heart, he approaches life with an optimistic outlook. His ultimate aspiration is to make films, combining his artistic talents to create visual masterpieces. Currently, Haque shares his expertise as an English Language and Literature teacher at the University of Creative Technology in Chittagong, Bangladesh.

Md. Ziaul Haque's legacy is one of unwavering creativity, inspiring individuals through his words, performances, and scholarly contributions. His ability to bridge gaps and push boundaries continues to leave an indelible mark on the world of literature and beyond.

List of His Books

Language/Translation:

1. Advanced Reading and Writing, The Easy Way [2011]
2. Advanced Reading and Writing: History, Developments, Concepts and Techniques [2014]
3. Prose Translation: Problems and Solutions [2017]

Poetry:

1. Give Me a Sky to Fly [2014]
2. Fragrance of Love [2014]
3. Hazrat Shah Jalal (R.A): Ekti Mohakabbo [Hazrat Shah Jalal (R.A): An Epic] [2015]
4. Poems of Love [2015]
5. Poetenry: Poems of Ten Lines [2015]
6. Kurine: Poems of Twenty Lines [2015]
7. A Farewell to Love [2016]
8. Do not 'FALL' in Love, 'RISE' in Love! [2017]
9. Haqueian Verse: A New Poetic Form [2017]
10. Fiverse: Poems of Five Lines [2018]
11. Sexual Poetenry: Poems of Ten Lines [2019]
12. Sexual Fiverse: Poems of Five Lines [2019]
13. Tennet: Poems of Ten Lines [2019]
14. Erotic Fiverse: Poems of Five Lines [2019]
15. LUV All Around [2019]
16. The Last Embrace! [2019]
17. The New Literary & Poetic Forms Created by Md. Ziaul Haque [2020]
18. Neel Preme Lin [2020]

19. A Wall of Love [2020]

20. Be the Sky! [2020]

21. Let the Universe Know [2020]

22. A New Tide of Love [2020]

23. My Queen You Are! [2020]

24. Kun Faya Kun: "Be" & 'It Is'! [2020]

25. You Talk Like Magic! [2020]

26. In the Name of Love [2022]

27. A Love So Pure [2023]

Religion:

1. Eastern Thoughts Islam, Hinduism, Buddhism and Beyond [2015]

Religion and Science/Philosophy:

1. Visions and Deaths: Trying to Reveal the Mystery behind the Extremely Unnatural Deaths [2016]

Short Story:

1. Hell Followed Him! [2015]

2. Characterless [2015]

3. Kivabe Manuske Pagol Banano Hoy? [How are the People Driven Mad?] [2019]

4. The Crimson Puzzle [2023]

5. The Hidden Treasure [2023]

6. The Lost Ruby [2023]

7. The Midnight Murders [2023]

8. Echoes of Death [2023]

9. Treasure Island [2023]

10. Unsolved Cases [2023]

11. Best Detective Stories [2023]

12. Silent Conspiracy [2023]

13. Ghost [2023]

14. Ocean's Mystical Creatures [2023]

15. The Mysterious Package [2024]

16. Love Stories! [2024]

17. Love Love! [2024]

18. Platonic Love Stories [2024]

19. Love Triangle [2024]

20. Symphony of Love [2024]

21. Unrequited Love [2024]

22. Exodus [2024]

23. Extramarital Love [2024]

24. Forbidden Love [2024]

25. Black Magic [2024]

26. Conditional Love [2024]

27. Children's Adventures [2024]

28. Cove Mystery [2024]

29. Psycho [2024]

30. Bloodlust [2024]

Literary Criticism:

1. The Shakespeare-mystery: Much Ado about Nothing [2015]

2. Othello's Murder [not suicide] by Iago! [2017]

3. Choice of Slurs in *Romeo and Juliet*: A Linguistic and Sociolinguistic Analysis [2024]

4. Power of Slurs in *Othello*: Speech Acts Explained [2024]

Children:

1. Rocket in My Pocket [2015]

2. Tom and Jerry [2016]

3. Rat in the Hat [2016]

4. Voyonkor Sublet **[Scary Sublet]** [2016]

5. Pokemon [2017]

6. Batman [2018]

7. The Lost Treasure [2023]

8. The Secrets [2023]

Songs/Lyrics:

1. Love Songs of Md. Ziaul Haque [2016]

Poestory [Poetry + Story]:

1. Poestory [Poetry + Story]: A New Literary Form Created by Md. Ziaul Haque [2017]

2. Md. Ziaul Haque Proneeto Golpita [Golpo + Kobita] [2020]

Essay/Article:

1. Not English, We Want a New International Language! [2018]

Quotes:

1. Famous Quotes of Md. Ziaul Haque [2020]

Novel:

1. Whispering Shadows [2023]

2. Silent Vengeance [2023]

Drama:

1. A Journey to Mars [2023]

2. **Hamlet: A Comedy [2023]**

Screenplays:

1. Romantic Screenplays [2024]

2. Supernatural Screenplays [2024]

3. Screenplays: Extramarital Affairs [2024]

4. Screenplays [2024]

5. Screenplays: For Short Films [2024]

6. Screenplays: Detective Genre [2024]

Get in Touch with Md. Ziaul Haque

E-mail
mdziaulhaque708@gmail.com

Website
kingofwords.uteach.io

Twitter
https://twitter.com/mdziaulhaque83

Facebook
https://www.facebook.com/zhaque1

YouTube
https://www.youtube.com/channel/UCRuvzlmvqeKTyig0vN2W49g

Facebook Fan Page
https://www.facebook.com/mdziaulhaque2014

Amazon
https://www.amazon.com/Md.-Ziaul-Haque/e/B00KENUD7S%3Fref=dbs_a_mng_rwt_scns_share

Blogger
blogger.com/profile/13860033902962538685

Foodeling BD
https://www.youtube.com/channel/UCmvjdHLbQ-W7OSX8p-MiIkg

www.ingramcontent.com/pod-product-compliance
Lightning Source LLC
Chambersburg PA
CBHW050035230526
45470CB00003B/1285